The SPORTS HEROES Library

World-Class
MARATHONERS

Nathan Aaseng

 Lerner Publications Company • Minneapolis

ACKNOWLEDGMENTS: The photographs are reproduced through the courtesy of: pp. 4, 7, 9, 17, 18, 22, 25, 30, 33, 35, 36, 43, 44, 46, 52, 53, 54, 57, 60, 62, 64, 70, 72, 76, 79, 80, Wide World Photos, Inc.; p. 39, Yale University; p. 74, University of Oregon.

Cover photograph: Peter Travers

To Howie Cook

LIBRARY OF CONGRESS CATALOGING IN PUBLICATION DATA

Aaseng, Nathan.
  World-class marathoners.

  (The Sports heroes library)
  SUMMARY: Outlines the history of the marathon and the careers of seven great marathon runners, including Emil Zatopek, Abebe Bikila, Frank Shorter, and Bill Rodgers.

  1. Runners (Sports)—Biography—Juvenile literature. 2. Marathon running—Juvenile literature. [1. Runners (Sports) 2. Marathon running] I. Title. II. Series.

GV1061.14.A18   796.4'26 [B] [920]   81-13660
ISBN 0-8225-1325-0   AACR2

Manufactured in the United States of America

International Standard Book Number: 0-8225-1325-0
Library of Congress Catalog Card Number: 81-13660

2 3 4 5 6 7 8 9 10 91 90 89 88 87 86 85 84 83

Contents

At the start of the 1980 Boston Marathon, thousands of runners make their way through Hopkinton, Massachusetts.

Introduction

A Frenchman named Lemeusieux took the early lead in the world's first official marathon in 1896. His coach rode a bicycle alongside to check on his runner's progress. At one point in the race, the coach actually veered into Lemeusieux and knocked him down! Eight years later, a South African faced an even more disheartening obstacle at the 1904 St. Louis (Missouri) Olympics. There he was chased off the marathon course by some fierce dogs. Forced to run a mile out of his way to avoid being bitten, he ended up in eighth place.

Those incidents give an idea of what early marathons were like. The marathon was a haphazard race. Runners were sent out on their own, and whatever happened to them between the start and finish was left to fate. Even the official length of the marathon came about because of a spur-of-the-moment idea. In 1908 the British royal family chose the lawn in front of Windsor castle as the starting line for that year's Olympic race. That starting point was selected simply because it would give the royal children a good view of the start. That made the race slightly longer than the original marathons. But the distance of 26 miles and 385 yards (42.2 kilometers) remains as the standard distance for the marathon race today.

While marathon runners are admired, they also have been suspected of being just a little bit crazy. The marathon has been thought of as the ultimate torture, and many could not understand why people would put themselves through such an ordeal. In fact, as late as the 1960s only a handful of runners would show up at the starting lines of marathon races.

But in the past decade or so, marathoning has changed completely. In the late 1970s, the sport's biggest problem was finding room for all who wanted to enter. The United States' oldest and most famous run, the Boston Marathon, began in 1897 with only 15 brave contestants. Today officials have been forced to set up qualifying standards in order to try and reduce the field to a workable number. At the starting line in 1980, the New York Marathon massed over 14,000 official entrants. There were so many racers that many did not reach the starting line until long after the race had started!

The marathon is no longer a lonely sport at such major events as the New York Marathon. Here race fans crowd the finishing chute to see Frank Shorter complete his victorious 1976 run.

People used to feel lucky just to survive a marathon. Now the top runners blaze through courses so fast that the average jogger could not keep up the pace for half a mile. The first Olympic marathon was run at an average speed of over seven minutes per mile. Now the lead runners speed through the entire race at better than a five-minute-per-mile clip. Top marathon runners do not try to conserve their strength anymore by running a smooth, even pace. Instead they try to break away from other runners with bursts of speed.

Women have also changed the sport considerably. Although denied official entry, there was a woman runner in the first Olympic marathon. Her name was Melpomene, and she ran the course in about four and one-half hours. For the next 70 years, however, women marathoners were not heard from again. At that time, it was widely believed that women could not safely run in such grueling races. In 1966 when Roberta Gibb Bingay asked to be included in the Boston Marathon, she was denied permission. So she hid in some bushes and "unofficially" entered the race. It was only after years of confrontation that marathons were opened up to women in the early 1970s. Now women race alongside the men as they battle for honors in their

Grete Waitz is well on her way to setting her third straight women's world record in the marathon. She finished this 1980 New York Marathon with a time of 2:25:41.

division. Given the chance to run, women such as Norway's Grete Waitz have proven their marathon ability. Waitz has run a time of 2:25:41, a time that would have won every men's Olympic marathon until 1952! And in the 1984 Olympics in Los Angeles, a marathon for women will be one of the officially approved events for the first time.

One thing that has not changed about the marathon is distance. More than 26 miles is still an *awfully* long way to run. And today's racers still experience "the wall" at about 20 miles. That is the

9

distance at which the human body begins to run out of energy. Marathoners have learned to combat this fatigue by making use of the refreshment stands located along the race course. These breaks, combined with advanced methods of training, have helped to push top runners to the brink of human endurance.

There is probably no one who has pushed himself harder in a race than Australia's Derek Clayton. In 1969 on a course in Antwerp, Belgium, he recorded a time of 2 hours, 8 minutes, and 34 seconds. While it is not fair to compare times of marathoners because of the varying amount of hills in each course, until 1981 that stood as the fastest time ever run in a marathon. As an indication of how hard Clayton pushed his body that day, he never completely recovered from the race and retired from running soon afterwards.

Why has such a demanding race—one that often pays no prize money—become so popular? One reason is that the jogging boom has gotten more people into running. Distance running has been shown to be an excellent way to keep fit. But perhaps even more important is the tremendous challenge that the marathon provides. For most people, the marathon is still the ultimate test of endurance and will. And here are some of the runners who have best met that challenge.

1
Early Marathoners

Nearly 2,400 years passed between the world's first and second marathon runs. According to legend, a Greek runner known as Philippides (or Pheidippides) ran the first race all by himself. That marathon was not part of the ancient Greek Olympic Games, and Philippides did not run it for sport. He was merely a messenger who was following his orders.

Along with his fellow soldiers in the Athenian army in 490 B.C., Philippides faced a desperate situation. A huge Persian army under King Darius was marching in to destroy their country. The Athenian general, Miltiades, marched his men to the Plain of Marathon to hold off the invaders. Seeing that the Persians greatly outnumbered the Athenians, Miltiades sent his great runner, Philippides, to recruit help from the city of Sparta. The journey to Sparta was about 300 miles round trip, blocked by rivers and mountains. Philippides, nevertheless, covered the distance in three or four days. But his heroic run was, unfortunately, a waste of breath. He reported that the Spartans would not be able to get to Marathon in time to help the Athenian army.

When the Athenians met the Persian army in battle, the people of Athens waited in a state of fear. Since the Athenians needed every man they could find, a tired Philippides probably had to join in the battle, too. In spite of the odds, the Athenians completely routed the Persians and chased them back to their ships.

According to tradition, Philippides was then called on to report the good news of victory to the worried city of Athens. Though he must have been exhausted, he set out on the 25-mile trip. There is no record of how fast he ran this distance, but the strain of the run in the hot September weather of Greece did him in. Philippides struggled to the city with his last ounce of strength. "Rejoice, we conquer!" he gasped. Then he died.

SPYRIDON LOUIS

In 1896 a French scholar named Michel Breal was

among those who tried to bring back a race patterned after the ancient Greek Olympics. Impressed by the legend of Philippides, Breal put up the cash for a silver cup to be awarded to the winner of an Olympic race in honor of the man. He proposed that the race follow the original course run by Philippides and be called the Marathon after the starting point of that ancient run.

The city of Athens was proud to host those first modern Olympics in 1896. But as the Games drew to a close, they were a little embarrassed because not a single athlete from Greece had won a first-place prize. Their last chance for victory was in the marathon.

Twenty-five starters lined up at the bridge of Marathon, ready to brave the 25-mile trip. Among them was Spyridon Louis from the nearby village of Marousi. Louis made a living by hauling water to and from Athens. Every day he loaded up his mule and jogged alongside during the 7-mile trip. After years at his job, Louis had developed a good deal of endurance.

Early in the race, Louis and his fellow Greek runners took their usual places near the rear of the pack. And for a long time a Frenchman, Lemeusieux, led. Then at about 18 miles, American Arthur

Blake took over. Meanwhile, horseback riders carried news of the runners' progress back to the crowded stadium in Athens, where fans kept hoping to hear that one of their countrymen was in the lead.

As the racers neared the city, many of the leaders had to slow down or drop out because of the heat. Finally at about the 23rd mile, Spyridon Louis took over the lead. When he trotted into the stadium toward the finish line, the fans went wild. Two of the royal princes ran down to the track to jog beside Louis and escort him to the finish. Just under three hours after leaving the bridge at Marathon, Louis hit the finish line and captured first place for Greece in the world's first marathon race.

FELIX CARVAJAL

The most colorful marathon figure of all time was probably Felix Carvajal, a tiny, penniless Cuban who suddenly decided to run in the marathon at the 1904 Olympics. Felix earned the money for his trip to the Olympics by running around a crowded square in Havana, Cuba, while people threw money at him. Even with that support, Carvajal nearly starved before he made it to St. Louis for the Olympics. Felix, however, was such a lovable fellow that he soon made friends among the other athletes. And they made sure he was well fed.

At racetime Felix displayed how little he really knew about distance running. It was a scorching hot day in St. Louis, and Carvajal strode to the starting line wearing a long-sleeved shirt, heavy trousers, and a pair of Oxford walking shoes. His new friends helped him by cutting off his sleeves and pants legs, but they could do nothing about his shoes.

Once the race started, Carvajal had the time of his life. He smiled and chattered at the racers and the spectators. Along the way, he kept an eye out for good-looking fruit. Felix swiped some peaches from a bystander and hopped a fence to get at some green apples. The apples, unfortunately, gave him stomach cramps, and Carvajal had to lie down for awhile until he felt better. But despite all of those delays, Carvajal not only completed the course—he finished fourth! Few of the other racers had been able to finish the race, and experts marveled to think how well Felix might have done if he had known anything about distance running.

PIETRI AND HAYES

For sheer drama and confusion, few events in sports match the 1908 Olympic marathon held in London, England. Throughout the Olympic contests, bad feelings between the American and the British teams had been flaring up. So when an Italian candymaker, Dorando Pietri, burst ahead of American Johnny Hayes to take the lead near the end of the marathon, British fans were delighted.

Dorando entered the stadium and headed for the finish line with what seemed like an unbeatable lead. But he had spent so much energy to gain the lead that he had literally run himself into the ground. Pietri stepped onto the track, turned in the wrong direction, and collapsed. Olympic officials pointed him in the right direction and helplessly looked on as he staggered forward, barely conscious.

By this time Johnny Hayes was entering the stadium. The British crowd screamed their encouragement to Dorando, pleading with him to keep going. Although his legs seemed to be made of lead, the little Italian gamely pushed on. He fell, tried to get up, and fell again. With Hayes closing in fast, Dorando stumbled again. The British officials could stand it no longer. They helped Dorando to his feet and half-dragged him across the finish line.

Dorando, of course, had to be disqualified, and the first place was awarded to Hayes. But the crowd was so moved by the Italian's valiant try (he was nearly killed by his effort) that they wanted to give him first prize anyway. They would have been even more upset had they known that Hayes was a professional runner who probably had no business being in the Olympics anyway. But the verdict stood, and Hayes is still in the record books as the victor of that dramatic race.

The crack of the starting gun at the 1976 Montreal Olympics begins another chapter in the colorful history of the Olympic marathon.

A gasping Emil Zatopek looks as though he has run his last step. But he not only beat his fresher-looking opponents in this 1952 Olympic 5,000-meter run—he also set an Olympic record.

2
Emil Zatopek

Emil Zatopek may have been the poorest judge of talent in track and field history. Born in Koprivnice, Czechoslovakia, in 1922, Emil went through all his growing years without realizing his running skill. In fact, he was considered a bookworm who did little at all in the way of exercise. Emil was already in his late teens and working at a shoe factory when his first running opportunity came. The factory had a fitness coach who told Zatopek to enter a race. Emil pleaded with the man to let him skip the race, claiming he was "too weak" to run for any distance. As it turned out, that was like Muhammad Ali claiming to be too shy to make a public appearance! The factory coach insisted that Emil give it a try. The youngster did well, and he went on to become the top distance runner in the world.

Once Emil discovered how well he could run, there was no stopping him. The boy who had once tried to avoid races now went out of his way to compete. He once rode his bike 180 miles to Berlin, Germany, to enter a 5,000-meter race, which he won.

When World War II swept over Europe in the 1940s, Zatopek had to continue his running career in the Czech army. Making the best of the situation, he ran workouts while wearing his heavy army boots. When the war ended, Emil stayed on in the army of the new Communist government.

Zatopek first gained international fame in the 1948 London Olympics, the first Olympics to be held after the war. When Emil saw athletes of all nations come together in peace, it seemed as if the world was having a new beginning.

Such thoughts made him feel so good that he could hardly wait to get started at his main event, the 10,000-meter run. In that race, he set such a quick pace that even the world record-holder in that event, Finland's Viljo Heino, was hard pressed to keep up.

Track experts watching Zatopek's performance were appalled and almost embarrassed. Emil's running form was probably the worst ever seen in world-class competition. Some writers wrote that he ran as if he had just been stabbed or poisoned. He chugged along with his elbows wide, eyes almost in tears, and a grimace on his face. Puffing, gasping, and moaning, he would sometimes clutch at his heart or his ribs. He was soon nicknamed "The Beast of Prague." Many of those actions were probably just for show, but they certainly caught the crowd's fancy in the 10,000-meter race. It seemed to spectators that Zatopek was running to his death and pulling the great Heino with him, too. Incredibly, Zatopek kept going faster and faster. By the end of the race, the crowd roared with every step he took. Heino finally gave up chasing Emil, and Zatopek staggered to the finish amid wild cheers. Besides winning the gold medal, he had set an Olympic record with a time of 29:59:06.

Over the next four years, the more the world found out about Emil, the more incredible he seemed. His workouts were simply superhuman. Emil liked to run a series of fast 400-meter dashes and then take a slow 400-meter jog between dashes to recover. Zatopek often repeated this until he had finished 60 tough 400-meter runs. There were even reports that when the Olympics drew near, Zatopek would step up the workouts to 90 fast dashes!

Emil refused to miss a workout for any reason.

In this 1947 race, Zatopek surges ahead of Finnish rival Viljo Heino.

When he had to stay home one evening, he filled his bathtub with dirty clothes, soap, and warm water. Then he switched on his radio and ran in place in the tub for the next two hours!

Taking a clue from the mailman's motto, Emil did not let snow or darkness keep him from his appointed workouts. After a heavy snowfall, he would stomp a trail in the woods near his home. At night he could be seen running on his trail, carrying a torch in his hand.

At the 1952 Olympics, Emil had a chance to show his courage in Finland, the home of the world's greatest runners. Led by Paavo Nurmi, the "Flying Finns" had dominated distance running for 20 years.

Emil, who had been promoted to army captain by this time, first went to work in the 10,000-meter run. Groaning and clutching, he sped to a gold medal with a time of 29:17, more than 40 seconds faster than his own Olympic record! A few days later, Zatopek went on to take the 5,000-meter run to set another Olympic record of 14:06:6.

Following this performance, experts conceded that Emil was one of the top runners of all time. But Emil was not through yet. After watching his wife set an Olympic record in the javelin event,

Emil broke the news. He would also enter the marathon. Emil impishly explained that after his wife's performance, he had to do something more to uphold his honor in the family!

No one knew what to expect from Zatopek in the marathon. He had never run one before, and he should have been exhausted from his other two races. With this in mind, Britain's fine marathoner, Jim Peters, set a fast pace. He wanted to force Zatopek to use up early in the race what energy he had left.

Despite the murderous pace, Emil enjoyed talking with his opponents. He was a language expert, so he could speak to many of the runners in their own languages. At about the halfway point in the race, Emil moved up next to the shoulder of Peters, who was leading. He asked Peters in English if perhaps they were not running a little faster than was wise. Hoping to break Zatopek's spirit, Peters calmly lied and said the pace was actually too *slow*.

Zatopek nodded and took off at an even faster pace. A few miles later, Peters, the pre-race favorite, was so wiped out he had to drop out of the race. Zatopek then glided easily through the rest of the course. His time of 2:23:03 broke the previous Olympic record by over six minutes.

Zatopek seemed to be enjoying himself more in the 1952 Olympics. An Olympic record of 2:23:03.2 in this marathon and two other gold medals gave him plenty to smile about.

After completing the top distance running performance in Olympic history, Zatopek was his usual outspoken self. "The marathon is a very boring race," he said.

Zatopek finished sixth in the 1956 marathon and retired two years later, a national hero. In the next 12 years, however, he turned from hero to disgrace. In 1968 Emil openly supported the new Czech government reforms. So when Soviet tanks rolled in to put a stop to the reform, Emil was singled out for scorn. The great Olympic runner was assigned to the job of garbage collector.

It was not that easy, however, to make the Czech people forget about Zatopek's thrilling runs in the 1952 Olympics. So many people recognized Emil and offered to help him at his job that he had to be taken off the garbage detail. Then Zatopek was assigned to a job inspecting insulation, where he would not be seen. Only by keeping him away from the public could the government stop Emil's countrymen from treating him as a hero.

3
Abebe
Bikila

There were smiles in the crowd as the marathon leaders came into view under the bright floodlights. It was the 1960 Olympics, and one of the runners was actually running barefoot over the hard streets of Rome! Onlookers must have wondered how long this unknown runner, slamming his unprotected feet on the pavement, could last against that top field of runners.

Even if the spectators had known the history of the barefoot competitor, they would not have given him much chance in the race. Abebe Bikila, born in 1932, was a poor boy from a mountain village in Ethiopia whose life had been changed by a single sight. On a trip to the Ethiopian capital of Addis Ababa, Abebe could not take his eyes off the splendid palace guard of Emperor Haile Selassie. He was so impressed by the guards that he stayed in the city, determined to become one of them.

Bikila got his wish and joined the guard as a lowly private. It was then that he was introduced to competitive running. He was singled out from the guards to train under the direction of Swedish coach, Ohni Niskanen. Running came naturally to Abebe, since that had been the only means of transportation in his home village. Yet at first Coach Niskanen saw little hope that Abebe could develop into a top runner. Bikila had skinny legs, poor running form, and a bad sense of balance when he ran. He made progress over the years, but he still placed no better than third in the Ethiopian Olympic trials for the 1960 marathon. Going into the Rome Olympics, Abebe was already 28 years old. So there did not seem to be much hope for him to improve very much.

At the Olympics, Abebe had not intended to run the marathon without shoes. The ones he had worn in Ethiopia had worn out, and he expected to find new ones in Rome. But none of the shoes he tried on felt comfortable. So rather than risk blisters by using poorly fitting shoes, Bikila decided to run barefoot. During the rest of his stay in Rome, he toughened his feet by running barefoot workouts.

The 1960 Olympic marathon was run in an inspiring setting. The race started at dusk to avoid the stifling midday sun. Torches and floodlights lit the entire course. From the start at a square designed by Michelangelo, the runners weaved through some of the ruins of ancient Rome. One stretch took them down the narrow Appian Way, a road that had been built by the Romans over 2,000 years ago. Running in the marathon was like running through the pages of history.

As the miles went by, the lead pack dwindled until only two runners remained in front. Abdesalem Rhadi of Morocco led the way with the barefoot Bikila hot on his heels. Both ran smoothly and easily, and they neared the finish almost stride for stride. But with less than a mile to go, Bikila drew away from Rhadi. Still strong at the finish, he pulled away to beat Rhadi by 25 seconds. His time of 2:15:16 had smashed the old Olympic mark by almost 8 minutes.

More important than Olympic records and personal goals, however, was the fact that Bikila had cleared the way for other African runners. Before his marathon victory, no black African had ever won an Olympic gold medal. Inspired by Bikila's effort, athletes from Ethiopia, Kenya,

Barefoot Abebe Bikila shocked the running world in the 1960 Rome Olympics. He wore down his final rival, Abdesalem Rhadi of Morocco, to claim victory in the last mile.

Uganda, and other countries now set out to become the world's best at their events.

Abebe did not allow his win to affect his life much. He kept his job as a member of the palace guard, and he still kept to himself, running his workouts and enjoying an occasional game of basketball or tennis. By the time the 1964 Olympics were about to begin in Tokyo, Japan, the track world knew little more about Bikila than they had before his surprise win in 1960.

Abebe's bid to become the first person ever to win two Olympic marathons received a terrible blow just a month before the Games began. Bikila had to undergo surgery to have his appendix removed. It seemed hopeless for him to recover from the operation and try to get back into running condition in such a short time.

Bikila, nevertheless, showed up at the starting line. This time he was dressed in white socks and in shoes that looked like boots compared to his thin legs. Alongside him were such great runners as Australia's Ron Clarke and Buddy Edelen from the United States. Edelen had been running so well that he almost singlehandedly had made marathoning a popular sport in the U.S.A. But as far as Bikila was concerned, he could just as well have been at the starting line by himself. For as little as the world's runners knew about Bikila, the Ethiopian knew even less about them. He had such confidence that he had not even bothered to find out who his opponents would be.

Over a million Japanese spectators lined the course to see the marathon race. Many of them saw Abebe take an early lead with his usual effortless gait, and he rounded the halfway post all by himself. From that point, it was just a matter of how wide the margin of victory would be. Abebe entered the stadium for the final yards of the race, breezed through the final lap on the track, and slapped down the finishing tape long before any competitors came into view.

After running a record time of 2:12:11, Abebe launched into some calisthenics, appearing as fresh as if he had just hopped out of the shower. Although he was doing it to keep his muscles loose rather than to show off, his headstands delighted the crowd. When his rivals finally finished, they called Bikila's run the greatest achievement in track history.

Abebe looked forward to the 1968 Olympics with even more enthusiasm. Those Games would be held in Mexico City at an altitude of over 6,000 feet.

Wearing shoes in Tokyo in 1964, Bikila easily outdistanced all of his rivals to win his second straight Olympic marathon.

While other runners would be struggling with the thin air, Abebe would find it no problem. After all, he was used to training in the mountains of Ethiopia at 8,000 feet above sea level. In the race, however, Abebe came down with an injury he could not overcome. His knee hurt him badly, and although he ran with the leaders for one-third of the way, the pain forced him to drop out. With Bikila out of the race, another Ethiopian runner, Mamo Wolde, finally had a chance to enjoy the spotlight and to win the gold medal.

A year later, Bikila was driving in Addis Ababa at night. Blinded by the headlights of an oncoming car, he veered off the road and overturned into a ditch. As a result of the accident, he was paralyzed from the waist down and had to watch the 1972 marathon from a wheelchair.

Abebe, however, remained a national hero to the people of Ethiopia. The trail to his small cottage was well worn from people coming to see the marathon champion. Before his death in 1973 at the age of 40 from the injuries he had suffered in the 1969 accident, someone had asked Bikila how he had been able to keep up his spirits after such a tragedy. Bikila calmly replied that success and tragedy were both a part of life and that one must learn to accept both. And there were few athletes who had been able to handle success and tragedy as well as Abebe Bikila.

Standing on the victory platform in Tokyo, the popular Bikila waves to the cheering crowds.

Frank Shorter gave American fans a treat they had not enjoyed in 64 years when he won the 1972 Olympic marathon in Munich, West Germany. The last American marathon winner had been Johnny Hayes in 1908.

Frank
Shorter

Every distance runner knows how it feels to be
yelled at by motorists and chased by dogs. But
things got so bad for Frank Shorter when he was
training for the 1972 Olympics that he risked his
life every time he went for a run. It all started
when Frank took time out during a run to help two
women who were being bothered by some men in
a jeep. The men did not appreciate Frank's inter-
ference, and from then on, he was a marked man.
He had to dodge ambushes and sprint away from
cars trying to run him down on the New Mexico
highways. Frank's dad finally had to drive behind
him with a shotgun during Frank's runs.

That incident probably could not have happened
to any other famous American sports star. But much
of Shorter's rise to stardom has been hard to believe.

Born in Munich, West Germany, in 1947, where his dad had been an army doctor, Frank had spent most of his childhood in the eastern United States, primarily in Mt. Hermon, New York. It was greed that had gotten Shorter interested in running. His parents gave him money to ride the bus to school, but Frank thought he could find a better use for the money. So he would often run the three miles to school and pocket the money instead.

Frank did not become interested in organized running, however, until his weakness for pie got the best of him. One day the cross-country coach offered pies to anyone in the school who could run four miles. Frank took up the challenge, and he beat everyone but the top five runners on the cross-country team. From then on, he started taking running more seriously.

Once Shorter finally put his mind to something, he rarely failed. For example, as a junior in high school, Frank was content to float around 80th in his class ranking. But when he realized that he would need better grades to get into the college of his choice, he studied harder and graduated in the top 10 in his class.

Shorter's running career was a similar story. At Yale University, his track performance was only

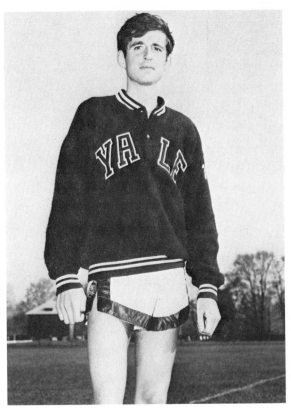

Frank in 1969 as a Yale senior, the year he suddenly emerged as a top distance runner

fair. He could run some competitive times, but he seldom won a race until the end of his senior year. Frank's classes had ended about six weeks before graduation. So with so much spare time on his hands, he decided to work harder on his running. After a few weeks of tough workouts, he entered the 1969 national meet for college runners. In one of the year's biggest surprises, Shorter took first place in the six-mile run.

After proving his running ability, Frank was ready to settle down to his studies at medical school. But somehow he could not resist the urge to see if he could run even better. So he left school and teamed up with another runner, Jack Bachelor, to train for important races. The two of them made an odd pair when they raced together. At 6 feet, 6 inches, Bachelor was one of the largest distance runners of all time. Shorter was only 5 feet, 10 inches, and he looked even smaller with his mosquito-like features. But the two would dominate American distance running for the next year.

In 1970 Frank was by far the top American six-miler. But even at that distance, European runners would simply keep pace with him and then out-sprint him at the end. So when marathoner Ken Moore suggested he try the marathon that year, Frank agreed. Shorter attempted his first marathon in the Pan-American Trials in 1971, and he finished second to Moore. Though Frank continued to run many shorter races after that, he knew that his best chance for an Olympic gold medal would be in the marathon.

Frank trained for the 1972 Olympics in Taos, New Mexico. It was there that he was nearly run off the road by the mysterious cars. But Frank refused to let anything get in the way of his training, and at times he would average as much as 200 miles during a week of hard running. The work paid off when Frank made the 1972 United States Olympic team in both the marathon and the 10,000-meter run.

In a way, the Olympics were a homecoming for Frank since they were held in Munich, the town of his birth. Unfortunately, four fast-kicking runners led by Finland's Lasse Viren spoiled his return and shut him out of a medal in the 10,000 meters. Some critics charged that Frank should have skipped that race and saved his strength for the marathon instead. Perhaps they were getting impatient with the United States' failures in the Olympic marathon, as it had been 64 years since an American had won the event. United States track fans wanted to see Shorter break that streak, and they did not want him to hurt his chances by running in other tough races.

But Frank was ready for the longer run, especially when he saw the weather report. It was a warm day, just the kind that most marathoners dread more than anything else. But Frank had an exceptional ability to stand up to the heat. He ran with the leaders from the very start of the race, keeping an eye out for Great Britain's outstanding runner, Ron Hill.

Anyone thinking the marathon was a matter of outlasting the competition at a steady pace had never seen Shorter race. For him the marathon was a race of surges, designed to break away from opponents. He said that there were many times during a race when a runner would feel good for a minute or two and then a few times when he could hardly lift his feet off the ground. Shorter's strategy was to take advantage of his "good" periods and set a furious pace. Somewhere during these bursts, he knew that his opponents would experience a bad stretch. If he could keep going hard then, he would be able to open a small lead on these runners. Shorter knew that the marathon was mostly a test of willpower. Therefore, if he could get others to give up staying with him for a few seconds, they would find it hard to regain their determination.

Frank started these surges in the early part of his Olympic race and set a brutal pace. Between 10 and 20 miles, he ran at a dangerously fast clip, and he did not know if he would have enough strength left to even finish the race. But his bursts had succeeded in breaking away from Hill and the rest. By the 20-mile mark, Shorter was well out

MARATHON
1014 SHORTER,F   USA
58 LISMONT,K   BEL
194 WOLDE,M   ETH
1001 MOORE,K   USA
558 KIMIHARA   JPN
289 HILL,R   GBR

The years of exhausting workouts have paid off for Shorter, who celebrates his Olympic win with teammate Ken Moore. Moore finished fourth.

in front. At that point he slowed, hoping he could save enough energy to finish. His plan worked perfectly, and he cruised into the stadium well ahead of the second-place finisher, Karl Lismont of Belgium. Frank's time of 2:12:19 gave him a comfortable two-minute victory.

43

Four years later in Montreal, Shorter set out to
defend his Olympic win. This time the weather was
not kind to him, and the runners were forced to
run in the rain. Although his muscles were tightening

Frank, whose fastest time ever was not fast enough to win the
1976 Montreal Olympic marathon, offers his weary congratulations
to Waldemar Cierpinski, the new champion.

up because of the rain, Frank again went into his dreaded spurts. This time one runner, Waldemar Cierpinski of East Germany, was able to stay with him. The German then broke away from Frank in the last six miles and captured the gold medal. Almost forgotten in the disappointment of defeat was the fact that Frank had run his best time ever— 2:10:45. (Cierpinski's time was 2:09:55.)

Although injuries and the United States' boycott of the 1980 Olympics kept him out of the spotlight, Frank continued to run. For over a decade he ran two workouts a day, almost without fail. And it had all started because Shorter had been curious about how well he could run. Because of his fine performances in the Olympics and other runs, now the whole world knows just how good he is. He is one of the very best.

Pumped up by the promise of victory, Cierpinski charges toward
the finish line in Montreal.

5
Waldemar Cierpinski

Critics of East Germany's government-run sports program have said that the East Germans are more like robots than athletes. They seem to be so programmed and so controlled, some say, that they take most of the fun out of sports. And the performances of the East German athletes in the 1976 Olympics in Montreal did nothing to quiet these arguments. Not only did they do incredibly well for a small nation, winning more gold medals than the United States, but they also seemed to be secretive and to lead rigid, controlled lives. Marathon runner Waldemar Cierpinski was mentioned as a prime example of the East Germans who have so dominated world athletics.

Waldemar was born in 1950 in Neugatterleben, a small East German town. As a youngster, he showed promise of being an exceptional runner, so he was transferred to a school in the large city of Halle. There he could receive top coaching to help him get the most from his natural ability. At first Waldemar excelled at the 3,000-meter steeple-chase, a race that included hurdles and a water jump. But even though he was national champion in that event, it was decided that he should switch to the marathon. His coaches reasoned that his short 5-foot, 7-inch stature and stiff running style would be a likely cause of injury in a race that used hurdles.

Waldemar was a quiet young man with a disciplined attitude toward running that made him popular with his coaches. Cierpinski had only to be told once what to do, and he would do it correctly and without complaining. By 1976 his hard work had brought him up to the level of some of the world's top marathoners. His best time going into the Olympics was 2:12:21, which was certainly competitive, if not spectacular.

With such men as Frank Shorter and Bill Rodgers of the United States and Jerome Drayton of Canada in the race, Cierpinski was completely overlooked.

And the news that Finland's Lasse Viren was going after his third gold medal of the Games by running the marathon further overshadowed Waldemar. Of course, not even Cierpinski thought he could outlast Viren and the rest. But as Waldemar watched his East German teammates haul in fistfuls of medals, he started to gain confidence. After all, he thought, if his teammates could win gold medals, why couldn't he?

The runners who took to the streets of Montreal on the day of the marathon were soon as soaked as the puddle-filled pavement. An off-and-on drizzle and 75 percent humidity soon had the competitors glistening wet. As expected, Shorter, Viren, Rodgers, and Drayton were all among the leaders through the first six miles. Then Shorter went into his spurts to break away from the rest. By the midpoint of the race, all of his major rivals had dropped back.

American track fans rejoiced as their television sets showed live pictures of Shorter out in front. The only one still challenging him was the East German, Cierpinski. Though he weighed only 128 pounds, the short-legged Cierpinski seemed chunky and awkward as he ran with Shorter. He certainly seemed no match for Frank, and fans sat back to wait for the American to finish off this last minor threat to his win. They expected Cierpinski to "hit the wall" at 20 miles, when the hard pace would finally take its toll.

Shorter did his best to lose his sideburned rival. For more than six miles, he put on bursts of speed. But the expressionless German hung on grimly. Shorter was beginning to feel the pain of the hard run, and his head bobbed to one side. Then suddenly, like a hunter running down a fox who had used up its bag of tricks, Cierpinski seemed to be in control. At 20 miles, Waldemar moved into the lead and pulled away from Shorter. Frank made one last effort to catch him at 25 miles, but Cierpinski glided easily away from him. By the time he entered the stadium for the finish, Waldemar was far in front. He seemed to fly around the track on his last lap, and then he kept going for an extra lap "just to be safe." But despite his fresh appearance, Cierpinski insisted that it had been a very hard race. He had pushed himself to a time of 2:09:55, more than two minutes better than his previous best.

During the next four years, many people wondered if Waldemar had been lucky in the Olympics. For as soon as the Games were over, he went back to being an average racer. Bothered by injuries, the best he could do was a fourth-place finish in the 1978 European championships.

But when it came time for the 1980 Olympics, Cierpinski suddenly came back to life. He blazed a 2:11 marathon in his country's Olympic trials to serve notice that he was ready to try for the gold again.

The large-scale boycott of the 1980 Olympics in Moscow greatly reduced the marathon field, and other than Cierpinski, there were no clear favorites. In the race, the Soviet Union's Vladimir Kotov led the way over his home course for the first half. He soon faded, however, giving way to Rodolfo Gomez of Mexico. Gomez stretched his lead to nearly 220 yards at one point but, like Kotov, he could not hold on to it. Then near the end of the race, Gerard Nijboer of Holland took over. Known as a fast finisher, Nijboer seemed in a good position to win the race. But Cierpinski finally made his move and roared down the stretch to catch the Dutchman. Blazing his final mile at such a speed that it seemed he had only used the previous 25 miles as a warm-up, he finished a half lap ahead of Nijboer in 2:11:03.

After his fabulous successes in the Olympics, one would have expected Cierpinski to become one of the top figures in the world of distance running.

With a comfortable win at Moscow in 1980, Cierpinski proves that his 1976 victory had been no fluke.

But Waldemar was so reserved and guarded in the few comments that he made to the press that he again faded mysteriously from the public eye. When he was not running, he liked nothing better than to quietly sit at home and listen to records. Having matched Abebe Bikila as the only two-time Olympic marathon champion, and setting his sights on a third title in 1984, one might say that Cierpinski was just as relaxed setting records as listening to them.

It's hats off to the winner as Bill Rodgers carries his to victory in the 1979 Boston Marathon.

6
Bill Rodgers

As a boy, Bill Rodgers enjoyed chasing butterflies to add to his collection. Later he found it more enjoyable to chase people. And he found them just as easy to catch, even without using a net! Already Rodgers' running skill has given him one of the largest collections of marathon wins in the world.

Bill was born in 1947 in Hartford, Connecticut, and grew up in nearby Newington, where he dabbled in distance running in school. He always did well enough to keep interested, but never so well that he attracted attention. He continued running at Wesleyan University, where he roomed with marathon runner Ambry Burfoot. Even the close contact with Burfoot, winner of the 1968 Boston Marathon, did little to inspire Bill. He avoided running marathons and even began smoking heavily, one of the worst things a distance runner could do. He left college with a master's degree in special education, and there was no reason to suspect that Rodgers would ever be heard from in the sport of running.

But in 1971 Bill lost his job at a Boston hospital, and he found himself with extra time on his hands. Rodgers, who had been running only for exercise, decided to try some serious, two-a-day workouts. By 1973 he felt ready to try the Boston Marathon. Boston, one of the world's most famous marathons, attracted top runners from all over the world. Every April for over 80 years, runners had gone out of their way to be able to take part in the race. Though Bill gave it a good try, he was not quite up to the challenge of the long race, and the 25-year-old Rodgers failed to finish.

That setback, however, made him even more determined to do well in distance running. By the following October, he had improved greatly and recorded a time just under two and one-half hours. In 1975 he returned to the Boston Marathon, this time looking to do more than just finish. He not only won the race, but he shocked experts by running a time of 2:09:55, the fastest time ever run by an American.

Rodgers has only a police escort for company as he wins his first Boston Marathon. Bill toured the course in that 1975 race in a time of 2:09:55.

That one race made Rodgers one of the favorites for the 1976 Olympics. In that race even though he was having trouble with the balls of his feet, Rodgers gamely kept up with the leaders for awhile. Then the discomfort finally forced him to fall back, and he finished in 40th place.

Such a crushing defeat in an important race again served to spark Rodgers to greater effort. It was as if someone had told him that he must win every race for the next few years to make up for his poor Olympic race. Bill trained hard and supported himself by selling running gear.

Rodgers' first chance for revenge on his marathon rivals came at the 1976 New York Marathon. That race had grown so fast in recent years that it attracted just as impressive a field of international runners as the Boston run. Bill won the race in 1976 and again the following year. It was an impressive double victory, but Bill was just warming up.

In 1978 the top distance runners in the world found that the only places up for grabs were second on down. That year Rodgers ran in 22 straight road races of various lengths without losing! Among his wins was another fine effort at the Boston Marathon. In that race, Bill, as usual, pulled out to an early lead. By that time, he was so used to winning that it must have been a shock when he peeked back over his shoulder during the final half-mile and saw a runner gaining ground on him. Rodgers had to push himself hard the final yards, and he managed to beat the charging Jeff Wells of Dallas, Texas. After racing for over 26 miles, Wells had come just three seconds short of beating Rodgers' time of 2:10:13.7.

Bill's many victories soon made him the world's most famous marathoner. Fans lining the race courses could spot Rodgers coming from far away, especially on a cold day. Rodgers, who loved to race in 40°F weather, always stood out from the other runners in the crowd in his fluffy stocking cap and gloves.

Bill had an unusual, floating style of running. His feet moved so quickly and so slightly that one competitor claimed he had never seen a picture of Bill racing in which either of his feet was touching the ground! Bill also built a reputation as an unbeatable downhill runner. Most racers look forward to the downhill portions of the marathon where they can let gravity pull them along. But running downhill against Rodgers was a nightmare. Trying to stay with him was like trying to keep pace with a runaway rollercoaster!

Bill's success continued in 1979 when he captured

On the way to his third Boston Marathon win, Bill's familiar stocking cap and gloves help to keep him warm.

his third Boston Marathon title. After a long battle with Japan's Toshihiko Seko, Bill surged to a 45-second win in an American marathon record of 2:09:27. Then Rodgers faced an even greater but more unusual challenge in the New York Marathon. The race was started with a countdown instead of the usual, "Take your marks, set, go." As the numbers were counted down, some antsy runners started moving forward early. Rodgers was unprepared for this and found himself caught in a crowd. It took him a mile to work his way into the top 150 runners. Halfway into the race, he still trailed fellow American Kirk Pfeffer by one and one-half minutes.

Rodgers continued to lose ground until about the 18th mile. Few runners win a marathon after losing contact with the leaders and trying to chase someone they cannot even see. But for Bill, chasing people was the most fun way to race. At the 23rd mile, he first spotted the lead truck guiding leader Kirk Pfeffer along the route. Bill stormed up a hill, went by the tiring leader, and coasted in for his fourth straight New York Marathon win.

Bill's hope of finally capturing an Olympic medal received a severe jolt in 1980. The United States decided to stay away from the 1980 Moscow Olympics in protest of the Russian invasion of Afghanistan. Rodgers was one of the most vocal critics of the boycott because he did not believe it was fair to use athletes for political reasons. He must also have known that at age 32 he would probably never again have as good a chance for a medal in the Olympics.

So it was a frustrated Bill Rodgers who ran the Boston Marathon in 1980. But not even the warm

Fans cheer on their hometown hero as Rodgers throws away his refreshment cup and heads for another Boston victory.

weather could slow him down as he took the lead early. His downhill charges soon helped him break free of his last rival, Kirk Pfeffer. With eight miles to go, Rodgers found he had used up about all the energy he had. But he kept going on sheer will-power. Fans lining the course helped him by cheering the local hero. They yelled and waved signs from sidewalks, rooftops and balconies.

Rodgers responded by holding on to his lead to win his fourth Boston Marathon in six years. But the following year, Rodgers lost to Toshihiko Seko in his bid to become the first runner to win the Boston Marathon four years in a row. Seko, who had placed second in the 1979 Boston race, broke Bill's record-setting marathon time by one second at 2:09:26. Rodgers finished third with a time of 2:10:34. Rodgers continued to run fine times in the early 1980s, but other, younger runners began to catch and pass him. After years of dominating the sport, Bill finally had to give up his position as king of the marathoners.

Rodgers' great record of 17 marathon wins through 1980 made it appear as if he had completely mastered the marathon. But Bill spoke of the race as if it were a worthy opponent. He would remember all too well races like the 1977 Boston Marathon. Although he was an experienced runner and in tremendous physical condition, Bill had to quit that race. As he says, the marathon can humble even the best runners. But it is a challenge that Rodgers always enjoys, and his love of marathoning has helped him win more of these races than any other runner in modern times.

The clock flashing over the finish line shows what Grete Waitz has accomplished in her very first marathon. The Norwegian is two seconds away from finishing the New York Marathon in a world record time for women.

7
Grete Waitz

Imagine a top female distance runner pushing herself near exhaustion in a race only to look up and see her opponent far off in the horizon ahead of her. It sounds discouraging enough to make a person quit the race. But for the past several years, most women runners have been thrilled just to catch a glimpse of Grete Waitz in a race. In most of her races, Waitz has been so far ahead that she has been well out of sight. So a runner who sees Grete near the end of a race knows she has done well. Waitz is so good at running that she is, in the words of Bill Rodgers, "off the charts."

Grete was born in Oslo, Norway, in 1953, the youngest of three children. Her next-door neighbor, Terje Pederson, got her interested in track and field before Grete was a teenager. Young Waitz was proud to say that she lived near Terje, who was the world record holder in the javelin in 1964. Pederson, in turn, was impressed by Grete's running, and he convinced her to join his track club. The neighbor certainly knew talent when he saw it. For by the age of 12, Grete had become Norway's top female runner.

At first Grete ran sprints instead of distance races, simply because there were no distance races for women. Track officials had long felt that women could not handle distance running. For many years, the longest women's event in the Olympics was the 200-meter dash. It was not until 1972 that the 1,500-meter run was added to women's Olympics, and even that distance is considered a middle-distance race. So it was not surprising that until she was 14, Grete thought of the 400-meter run as a long race.

But after finding herself unable to match the top European sprinters, Waitz moved up in distance. After a few years, she found herself to be strongest in races 3,000 meters or longer, which had then started to be more popular among women. Because of her success at those distances, many of her friends expected her to do well in the Olympics. They did not realize there were still no Olympic races for women at those distances. Instead Grete did her best in the longest Olympic run available to her—the 1,500 meters. She competed for Norway in both the 1972 and 1976 Games, but she did not win a medal. Many unknowledgeable fans considered her Olympic efforts a failure, and their comments hurt Grete. So she was glad when the Olympics were over, and she could go back to more comfortable events.

Waitz held a job as a schoolteacher, and she had to work her training around that job. So she got up at 6 A.M. to be on the roads before the cars were out. Then when she finished her school day, she would sleep an hour and later run her afternoon workout. During the summer, she especially liked doing her speed work on forest paths. She had no coach, only her husband and a brother who ran along with her as best they could.

In most of her races, Waitz's opponents had no better success staying with her than her running partners did. One 3,000-meter indoor race was thrown into confusion because Grete was so far ahead. Waitz was running a record pace when the lap counters lost track of how many laps she had run. So Waitz was forced to run an extra lap. But even then she passed the 3,000-meter point seven seconds under the old indoor record! As tough as she was on a track, Grete was even tougher in cross-country and road races, and she has seldom lost an off-track race.

Grete did not start marathoning until 1978. Actually she only agreed to enter the New York Marathon that year because it would be a good excuse for her to visit New York for the first time. She did nothing special to train for the race, and she hoped for a time of around 2:40. Because she had no experience at the race, she decided to run with Christie Vahlensieck of West Germany, who held the women's world record at 2:34:47.5.

The strategy seemed to be working as Vahlensieck led Waitz through the first half of the race at a comfortable pace. By that time, Waitz had found out what she needed to know about a marathon pace, and she passed up her rival. The expression "beaten by a mile" was an understatement for Grete's opponents in that race, as the Norwegian finished *nine* minutes ahead of the second-place finisher! Her time of 2:32:30 easily broke Vahlensieck's record and, most astounding of all, she had run the second half of the race faster than the first. (Vahlensieck did not finish the race.)

But Waitz did not have time to stay and discuss her performance. Instead she rushed back to

Norway so she would not miss a day of school.

The next year Grete returned to the New York Marathon. Just as before, she refused to train for the event, and preferred to concentrate on her 3,000-meter workouts instead. This time she tore through the first half of the course in 1:14:51. Quite a few eyebrows were raised when that time was announced. If Grete could hold the pace she would be the first woman to break two and one-half hours. Again Grete kept building up speed as she ran. Her second half was two minutes faster than her first, giving her a 2:27:42 world record!

In 1980 Waitz was starting to tire from her heavy schedule of races when she injured her heel. Her injury turned out to be a blessing in disguise as it forced her to cut back her training and gave her a much-needed rest. After taking it easy for awhile, Grete felt fresh when she flew to New York for her third marathon.

Race day was chilly, with strong winds threatening to slow down the runners. Grete, as usual, cruised through the course far ahead of the other women. She seemed to be able to concentrate so much on her running that she did not even notice all of the photographers aiming cameras at her or the male runners who were trying to stay with her.

Another race, another record. Grete's third marathon ends in a third
world record.

Also in the race was a strong American competitor, Patty Lyons-Catalano. Patty broke the American record for women in the race, finishing a few seconds under 2:30. It was a fine performance, but it did not even come close to matching Waitz, who set another world record at 2:25:41.

The first sign of competition in women's marathoning came suddenly in 1981. That year New Zealand's Allison Roe approached Grete's record with a 2:26:45 win in the Boston Marathon and then broke it with a 2:25:29 win in the New York Marathon. (Waitz did not complete that race because of shin splints.)

Although she was no longer the record holder, Waitz put on an impressive show to regain the New York title in 1982. Despite having to battle a tough wind, she toured the course in a fine 2:27:14. Next on April 17 in London, Grete set out to recover her world record. She broke the tape one second ahead of Roe's mark, but it was later determined that she had only tied it. Then the very next day in the Boston Marathon, Joan Benoit from Massachusetts helped to erase the controversy when she took over the record with a startling 2:22:42. Although women runners were catching and even passing the great Norwegian runner, they had to admit it had been Grete Waitz who had shown that it could be done.

Alberto Salazar makes good on his stunning prediction with a victory in the 1980 New York Marathon—his first race ever at that distance.

8
Alberto Salazar

Alberto Salazar had learned the value of long-distance travel at an early age. He was born in 1958 in Havana, Cuba, where his father was an early supporter of Fidel Castro. But within two years, Alberto's father had changed his mind about Castro—who had become the Cuban premier in 1959—and the Salazars had to flee the country. The family took a long trip, and finally ended up in a completely different climate in Wayland, Massachusetts.

Alberto learned another kind of long-distance travel from his older brother, Ricardo. After Ricardo began running long distance in school, Alberto decided to give it a try, too. Before long the younger Salazar passed Ricardo, and he went on to win praise as one of America's top high school distance runners.

As a University of Oregon student, "slow" runner Salazar sets a brisk pace to wear out his faster rivals.

For someone who loved running as much as Alberto did, it was not surprising that he chose to travel across the country to attend the University of Oregon. That school, located in Eugene, Oregon, is considered by many to be the track capital of the United States. Eugene has never experienced the "loneliness of the long distance runner." Fans there crowd into the stands to cheer and to give standing ovations to top runners. They can sense when a good race is being run, and they help urge runners on to record times.

Alberto's main problem in track at Oregon was a very serious one. He was a slow runner. World-class distance runners almost always have above-average speed at all running events. But Salazar could not run a quarter-mile faster than 57 seconds, a time that would not win a spot on most high school teams. To make up for this lack of speed, Alberto had to work hard. In races he was forced to lead from the start. Even in the six-mile run, he had to keep a fast pace so he could lose the fast finishers before the end of the race. In practices he knew he had to run more miles than anyone else.

Alberto was warned about working his body too hard, but he refused to let up. Finally, during his senior year of college in 1980, he came down with a bad case of tendonitis. The former workaholic despaired as he sat out workouts because of legs that were too sore to even jog. He tried all kinds of doctors and cures, but nothing seemed to work. Alberto talked of quitting, and he finally packed his bags for home.

Had he known the story of distance runner Alain Mimoun, Salazar might not have lost hope so soon.

After injuries threatened his running career, it seemed that Alain Mimoun (right) would be only remembered for his valiant losses to Emil Zatopek (left). But at age 36, a startling comeback gave him an Olympic gold medal in his first marathon.

Mimoun was an Algerian who had run under the flag of France in the 1950s. Only the presence of Emil Zatopek had kept him from being the world's top runner. Alain had finished second to Zatopek in three Olympic races.

After the 1952 Olympics, Mimoun developed a condition called sciatica that seemed to finish his career. Nothing in the medical world seemed to be able to help him run again. Then in 1955 Mimoun went on a pilgrimage to the Basilica of St. Theresa. After the visit, he was suddenly able to run again. At the age of 36, he entered the 1956 Olympics to run his first marathon. Even longtime rivals such as Zatopek were thrilled when Alain won the gold medal with a time of 2 hours, 25 minutes.

In Salazar's case, it was a trip he did *not* take that got him back on the track. Just as Alberto was starting for home, a car slammed into the back of his automobile. With his car broken, Alberto had to stay in Eugene. While he was there, he tried to jog again, and he was relieved to find that there was almost no pain. Slowly he regained his strength, and he set his sights on the 1980 U.S. Olympic trials that summer. Alberto placed third in the 10,000-meter run to win a place on the team. But because of the United States' boycott of the Games, he had to miss the Olympics.

Later that summer, Salazar entered the New York Marathon to see how he would do at a race where speed was not as important as endurance. Alberto confidently predicted he could run a time of 2:10.

This prediction upset many top runners, who thought he was making light of the race. Salazar nearly had to back away from his statement when he pulled a hamstring in training. But he recovered quickly enough so that he could still run the race.

Alberto was one of more than 14,000 official entries who bunched together at the starting line on October 26, 1980. For the first part of the race, he stayed back in a pack of runners, letting the more experienced men set the pace. Though the temperature was a chilly 45 degrees, made even more biting by a stiff wind, Salazar ran much of the way wearing only his sleeveless Oregon track uniform.

His main rival, Bill Rodgers, tripped and fell during the middle of the race and lost contact with the leaders. Before long others were dropping off the pace until only two runners were left battling for the lead. Rodolfo Gomez of Mexico and Alberto Salazar kept up their duel for mile after mile with neither giving any ground. Gomez then slowed down for a drink of water at the 21-mile mark. Salazar took advantage of this pause to try and break away from his rival. He reeled off a 4:52 mile into a strong wind to open up a lead over Gomez. Though his entire body ached the last mile, Salazar clung to his 30-second lead to claim the victory.

Salazar steps up an already grueling pace in an effort to pull away from Mexico's Rodolfo Gomez. It was Alberto's burst of speed at the 21st mile mark that finally opened up the lead to give him the win in the 1980 New York Marathon.

Salazar and Grete Waitz wear the wreaths given to the victors of the 1980 New York Marathon. Salazar repeated his win in 1981 with a record-breaking 2:08:13 and continued his amazing success in 1982 with a two-second win over Dick Beardsley at Boston and a four-second, third straight victory in New York against Rodolfo Gomez.

Marathon experts were not only stunned by the first-time marathoner's win, but also by his time. Salazar's 2:09:41 clocking was the seventh fastest marathon ever run! It was a race every bit as impressive as Mimoun's first try in the 1956 Olympics. There was, however, one major difference. Mimoun's marathon was the final chapter in a great career. For the 22-year-old Salazar, his incredible marathon run was only the beginning.